Egerton Ryerson

Laura Damania

Fitzhenry & Whiteside Limited

GO 1864

Contents Chapter

The Author

Laura Damania is a Toronto historian, author, and editor. For many years she was associated with The Ryerson Press.

FC
3071.1
.R93
D343
1975

For Shiawax

©1975 Fitzhenry & Whiteside Limited
    150 Lesmill Road
    Don Mills, Ontario, M3B 2T5

Printed and bound in Canada.

ISBN 0-88902-212-7

Ryersons Chapter 1

*When I had attained the age of eighteen, the Methodist
minister in charge of the circuit which embraced our
neighbourhood, thought it not compatible with the rules of
the Church to allow . . . the privileges of a member without
my becoming one. I then gave in my name for membership.
Information of this was soon communicated to my Father,
who, in the course of a few days, said to me: "Egerton, I
understand you have joined the Methodists; you must either
leave them or leave my house." He said no more, and I well
knew that the decree was final. . . . The next day I left
home. . . .*

Egerton Ryerson had a happy childhood. He was one
of a big loving family of nine children and had five
brothers and three sisters. Egerton was the fifth of the
six sons and, although there was a difference of twenty
years between the birth of the eldest child, George,
and the youngest, Edwy, the age gap—particularly as
they grew up—was unimportant. His brothers were
very close to him always and, of them all, William and
John were the dearest.

*The earliest United Empire
Loyalists were housed in camps.
This sketch of an encampent at
Johnstown, Ontario, in 1784 is
by a British Army officer*

Who were the United Empire Loyalists? Why did they emigrate to Canada?

Egerton was born on March 24, 1803 near the village of Vittoria in the township of Charlotteville, in Norfolk County, Ontario. His parents were Joseph and Mehetabel Ryerson, both United Empire Loyalists. The Ryersons had been settled in North America for two hundred years before the birth of Egerton. They were of Dutch Protestant origin, being descended from Martin Reyerzoon who had come to New York when it was still called New Amsterdam. The family name became Reyertz, Reyerse and, finally, Ryerson. (In maps of early Ontario settlements, it is spelt Ryerse and Ryersee.) Joseph Ryerson's elder brother Samuel, however, spelt his name Ryerse because that was how it was written on his army commission. No doubt he found it simpler to change his name than the commission.

The Ryersons had flourished in New Jersey until the outbreak of the American War of Independence. Because they took the British side, life then became difficult for them and they, like thousands of others, decided to seek their fortunes in British North America. For the sake of their convictions, they were prepared to give up everything and start all over again in a new country. They faced a hard decision and a tough future. In 1783, the brothers Samuel and Joseph emigrated to New Brunswick where, as Loyalists, they were eligible for grants of land. Samuel later moved to Upper Canada, where he made his home in Long Point Bay on the shore of Lake Erie, where Port Ryerse still commemorates his name. In 1798, Joseph and Mehetabel Ryerson and their six eldest children joined him in Upper Canada.

Joseph Ryerson was an attractive personality. When only fifteen years old and still under-age, he had talked himself into the Prince of Wales' Regiment in order to be with Samuel. He regarded service to the community as a duty. Only two years after his arrival in Upper Canada he was appointed high sheriff of Norfolk County. The high sheriff was responsible for jails, the appointment of jailers, and the selection of jurors. He also had to attend court sessions. Colonel Ryerson held the conventional ideas of his time and class: loyalty to king, church and country. He was a staunch Anglican.

The graves of Colonel Samuel Ryerse and his wife in the family burial plot at Port Ryerse

Though he was not a father his children could argue with, he inspired affection as well as respect.

Mrs. Ryerson lived for God and her family — probably in that order. Hetty, as she was called, had been a light-hearted, auburn-haired beauty of nineteen when she married Joseph. She was a Presbyterian, but became a Methodist in 1816. Her influence upon her children was profound, and five of her six sons became Methodist ministers. In an autobiography written in his old age, Egerton acknowledged his debt to his mother for "any studious habits, mental energy, or even capacity or decision of character." He also described what he called his "first religious impression." When he was five years old, "having done something naughty," his mother took him into her bedroom. He did not get the spanking he may have expected. Instead, his mother put her arms around him, told him how bad he had been, and prayed for him. He never forgot this.

Colonel Joseph Ryerson's house, near Vittoria

Twenty-five years after this incident, Mrs. Ryerson wrote a revealing letter to Egerton, then in York (Toronto). She said that she was well but prepared to die when God willed; she begged him to believe firmly, pray fervently, work abundantly; she sent his wife her love and an appeal to live a holy life. Then came the double-barrelled postscript:

"P.S. I observed in the *Guardian* an advertisement stating that a small seal skin trunk had been left at the York Hotel in december last containing wearing apparel and if not relieved in 3 weeks from the 19th of Feb. it would be sold to pay charges. Mr. Harris thinks William took them both [sic] on board the Steam Boat.
I have a crock of Butter; if you know of any chance of sending it, let me know of it."

She had no doubts about priorities.

Ryerson was fortunate not only in his family life. Luckily for him, the London and District Grammar School at Vittoria was only half a mile from his home. Even more fortunately, the master, James Mitchell, was a scholar who taught young Egerton English grammar and gave him a wider outlook than he could otherwise have received. Mr. Mitchell was probably also the "kind friend" who later gave the teen-ager his first Latin grammar and books on logic.

When he was fourteen, Egerton's father allowed

The Steamboat and Stage House, a pioneer Vittoria hotel built in 1805

him to leave home for a short while to attend "a course of instruction in the English language" given by two visiting professors, in which the boy distinguished himself. This was followed by a second course, during which one of the professors became sick. His colleague secured Colonel Ryerson's permission for Egerton to be the assistant teacher, a unique compliment to the boy's ability. What he heard and learned from these two able men first stimulated his love of books, his curiosity and his ambition.

Egerton was strong and healthy, and had been brought up to work with his hands. His father was a pioneer farmer who needed all the help he could get to survive. So although formal education was recognized as necessary and desirable, it came second to work on the land. This training—and also his naturally hardy physique—was to stand Egerton in good stead all his life.

Egerton was too young to fight in the War of 1812, although his father and three elder brothers saw active service. After the war, in 1815, these brothers, George, William and John, became deeply religious and gave up their Anglican faith for the Methodist ministry. They were too old for their father to do much about it.

At the same time, Egerton had a religious experience, known as "conversion," which was essential for anyone professing Methodism. Egerton Ryerson's conversion came after he had a vision of Jesus Christ approaching his bed. This changed him entirely, he later wrote:

"I henceforth had new views, new feelings, new joys, and new strengths . . . . From that time I became a diligent student, and new quickness and strength seemed to be imparted to my understanding and memory. While working on the farm I did more than [an] ordinary day's work, that it might show how industrious, instead of lazy, as some said, religion made a person. I studied between three and six o'clock in the morning, carried a book in my pocket during the day to improve odd moments by reading or learning, and then reviewed my studies of the day aloud while walking out in the evening."

Because of Colonel Ryerson's strong and entirely unconcealed prejudice against the Methodists, Egerton did nothing further for several years. However, by the time he was eighteen, he had to come to a decision, and he made his choice. His father turned him out of the house.

But Ryerson had also made plans. On the day he left home he went back to his school as an usher — the usual name at that time for an assistant teacher. Actually, he was a student-teacher, and while he worked hard with his pupils he taught himself too, by reading Latin, Greek, philosophy, politics and law. He made progress and was happy.

His father was not. Colonel Ryerson had taken the departure of his chief labourer badly. He blamed not only his son but also the Methodists for robbing him of that son's help on the farm. Although an usher earned very little, to help his father Egerton paid for a hired man to take his place. But this did not satisfy the Colonel either. Apart from his wounded feelings and although the hired man was a good worker, he could not help seeing that production fell. So, at the end of two years Joseph Ryerson came to see his son, "uttering the single sentence, 'Egerton, you must come home,' and then walked away."

Egerton had a healthy temper and his first impulse was to refuse. After all, he felt his father had been unjust to turn him out of the house merely because he was a Methodist. But for that very reason — to show

The word "prejudice" comes from the latin prae *(before)* judicium *(judgement), and usually means an unfavourable, irrational opinion. Do you think that Colonel Ryerson's dislike of Methodism is similar to any prejudice you know of? What are some causes of prejudice?*

what it meant to be a Methodist—he swallowed his anger and went home for a year.

He did the work of two men on the farm, at the same time keeping up with his reading as best he could. This behaviour considerably altered his father's attitude, both to him and his religion, and Colonel Ryerson asked his son to stay permanently on the farm.

Young Ryerson refused. Although he did not yet know what his career would be, he wished to continue his education in preparation for the future. He decided to move to Hamilton for a year to study at the Gore District Grammar School, whose headmaster was John Law. At Hamilton he lodged at the house of a family called Aikman.

In the 19th century, the study of Greek and Latin was essential for those wishing to pursue a university degree. Why was this so? Why, do you think, has this changed?

Ryerson went to Hamilton prepared to work hard and to learn as much Greek and Latin as possible. For this, he was ready to give up all other interests and relaxations. He loved music, but a week after his arrival he noted briefly, "I have not a moment to play on the flute." He went too far and overworked to such an extent that Mr. Law warned him that his health would suffer.

The warning went unheeded. At the end of six months Ryerson had a breakdown, developed pneumonia, and was not expected to live. In this extremity he vowed that, should he recover, he would become a minister and devote his life to his church. Slowly, he did get well, and even though Colonel Ryerson begged him to come home and even offered him a part share of the farm, his mind was made up.

At last, his father accepted the inevitable. With a sigh, he said, "Egerton, I don't think you will ever return home again." It was the first of many victories.

Methodists Chapter 2

The eighteenth century in Europe was an age of
scepticism. In England, however, the same period also
produced a great religious revival: Methodism. Among
the many brilliant men who led this movement, the
most famous was John Wesley, so much so that
Wesleyan came to be a synonym for Methodist. John
Wesley, his brother Charles, and their colleagues
travelled from town to town and from village to village,
preaching a new gospel to people who led poor and
sometimes hopeless lives. The Wesleyan doctrine of
salvation through conversion, with its promise of a
changed life on earth and eternal bliss after death, was
indeed evangelism, literally "good news," and the
movement spread like a forest fire.

*Can you name any religious
movements flourishing today
that might be compared to
eighteenth-century Methodism?*

John Wesley

Epworth Old Rectory, John Wesley's home in Lincolnshire, England, was haunted for a year in 1715-16. "Old Jeffrey" became a famous ghost and has often been written about. The house still stands and the visitor can see Jeffrey's room

A Methodist camp meeting in the United States. Someone in the foreground has been overcome by emotion

Methodist meetings were totally uninhibited. The preacher who, with voice, eyes and gestures, commanded sinners to repent while there was still time, who described with equal vividness the bliss of God's love and forgiveness and the horrors of hell, electrified those who heard him. People who felt that God had suddenly entered their lives did not behave with the decorum demanded at an Anglican service. They wept, danced, flung themselves on the ground, and praised the Lord with all the force of their lungs. In class-conscious England, this unseemly lack of self-control was regarded as "enthusiasm," what today would be called fanaticism. Worse, it was considered ill-bred.

Apart from that, Methodist doctrines themselves were distasteful to most people of education and rank. An aristocrat—admittedly a duchess—wrote: "It is monstrous to be told, that you have a heart as sinful as the common wretches that crawl on the earth." To a duchess, it was not only monstrous but impertinent. When the Countess of Huntingdon actually became a Methodist, it was far more than a nine-day wonder. She was nicknamed "The Queen of the Methodists" and considered a freak. Others were less fortunate; a naval officer threatened to send his Wesleyan wife to a madhouse.

It took time for the new teachings to penetrate beyond the "lower classes," to gain a wider acceptance. Colonel Ryerson, with his social and religious background, would naturally detest Methodism. And in his case there was an additional objection: he was ardently pro-British; the movement had a strong American element.

It was inevitable that Methodism should cross the Atlantic. John Wesley himself, as a young man, had gone to Georgia on a mission to the Indians. This was an unhappy experience, but others followed him with more success. In 1772, Wesley appointed a general superintendent of the "circuit" that was so soon to become the United States of America. Twenty years later, with the abolition of the Anglican Church as the established religion in America, membership had increased to 13,000 and was growing.

In Canada, one of the first Methodist missionaries arrived in the Maritimes from Yorkshire, England. Some of the British soldiers who came to the defence of Quebec City during the American War of Independence were of the same faith. Still more Methodists emigrated with the United Empire Loyalists. By 1791, the first circuit was established in Upper Canada.

The early missionaries, or circuit riders, were heroes. Carrying their few possessions in their saddlebags, they rode hundreds of miles, braved extreme hardships, even risked their lives, to reach the Indians and those settlers from Europe and the British Isles who had made their homes in tiny, isolated communities in the wilderness. These saddlebag preachers had no fixed homes, were dependent on their co-religionists for food and shelter, and received a salary of $100 to $200 a year.

On his twenty-second birthday, Egerton Ryerson wrote in his diary that he had decided to become a travelling preacher. This resolve soon became reality. His brother William, who had been working for two years on the Niagara Circuit, became seriously ill. The presiding elder and two of the circuit stewards visited Ryerson and asked if it would be possible for him to take William's place. He was ecstatic—and horrified.

A circuit rider

His first reaction was to make excuses: he had not yet fully recovered from his own illness; he could not afford the necessary horse and equipment. One of the stewards offered him a horse; the other said he would provide him with a saddle and bridle. As Ryerson said, "I then felt that I had no choice but to fulfill the vow which I had made. . . . "

He had little time to brood on the ordeal. He preached his first sermon on Easter Sunday, which that year was on April 3. He was so nervous that at least one person present noticed him trembling. This was only the beginning. In spite of his early physical and mental labours, Ryerson had always led a comparatively comfortable life. Now he had to adjust to the hardships and humiliations faced by a Methodist minister. He needed all his strength and fortitude. On one Sunday in the following month, he rode nearly 30 miles, preached three sermons, and instructed two classes. "I felt very much fatigued." Once he faced near-disaster: his mare wandered off and Ryerson spent two frantic days searching before he found her. He was lucky; sometimes cruel ill-wishers maimed missionaries' horses. No wonder that in those early days his diary reads like a fever chart. At one point he almost decided to return home, but his courage returned. He was able to stick it.

As well as preaching and travelling, ministers were expected to spend a part of each day studying. To fit in his reading, more often than not Ryerson had to do it on horseback. Not surprisingly, he went to bed at the latest at ten o'clock and got up at five.

In August, at the annual Methodist conference, Ryerson was admitted on trial to the Yonge Street Circuit, which covered a large area including York. He found the work hard, the lodgings primitive, and the roads "bad beyond description." This was a statement not a complaint, because the welcome from the people made up for everything. "We were received as angels of God."

Three months earlier, at a camp meeting attended by some Mississauga and Mohawk Indians, Ryerson had first met and been impressed by Peter Jones, a remarkable man of his own age who was already making a name for himself as a preacher. Jones

The Reverend Peter Jones was ordained in 1833 and spent his life in the Methodist ministry. With the help of his brother John, he translated the Gospels of St. Mark and St. Matthew into Chippewa

In London, in 1833, Ryerson called upon the Earl of Ripon "to enquire about the medal promised by His Majesty, William IV., to Peter Jones . . ." He is wearing the medal in this protrait

was the son of Augustus Jones, a United Empire Loyalist of Welsh extraction, and his wife Tuhbenahbenahneequay, the daughter of an Ojibway chief. Peter Jones and Ryerson were to work closely together and become lifelong friends. Jones accompanied Ryerson on his travels and sometimes acted as interpreter when Ryerson visited Indian settlements. He did so increasingly from 1826, when he was appointed missionary to the Credit River Indians.

At that time there was an Ojibway settlement by the Credit River, where the government planned a village. In fact, the cottages had been built on the higher ground when Ryerson arrived but the people were still living in wigwams near to the river. So he lived in one too, sleeping on a plank bed and feeling happy and comfortable. "I showed the Indians that I could work and live as they worked and lived." He also learned something of their language, so that after some months he "spoke in Indian" for the first time and said the Lord's Prayer in Chippewa.

Ryerson was a fast worker. After morning service on the first Sunday, he asked the congregation to contribute towards the cost of building a combined church and school. They gave generously from what they earned from the sale of handicrafts. Then Ryerson engaged a carpenter-mason, and himself went round his old circuit and to all his friends, as far as Hamilton, asking for money to make up the balance. In six weeks the house was built and paid for.

The first Methodist Church in York

Ryerson, however, had come to the Indians not merely to convert them to Christianity. He wanted to help them materially too. The Indians had helped the first European settlers materially — by teaching them the art of planting corn. But now, generations later, many Indians subsisted mainly on money earned by bartering furs and handicrafts. Some tribes had completely lost their touch for the land. First, he showed them how to make fences and gates for their gardens. Then he chose four men and worked with them individually, showing each in turn how to clear and plough his land and plant his first wheat and corn fields. The experience gained on the farm at home was now put to good use. In the evenings he got the schoolboys to help him cut, pile and burn the brushwood in and around the village. The children enjoyed the chore as long as Ryerson was there to keep an eye on them; once his back was turned, they stopped work and started to play around.

Give the arguments for and against trying to change some one else's religion. What is your point of view?

During this time, William Ryerson paid his brother a visit. He arrived during Operation Brushwood and "found Egerton about half a mile from the village, stripped to the shirt and pantaloons, clearing land with between twelve and twenty of the little Indian boys.... " He was highly delighted with everything that he saw and said so in a letter to their eldest brother George. He was specially pleased with the children's progress in spelling, reading and writing.

Sometimes Ryerson preached with more fervour than tact. During one of his trips to the Indians of Lake Simcoe, he spoke about the superiority of the Christians over those who worshipped "images". Some Roman Catholic fur traders from Lower Canada (Quebec) who were present looked very angry and started "muttering." But Ryerson had not the least intention of being tactful. He considered the traders, who ruined the Indians with whiskey, as one of the chief obstacles to progress, and had some harsh things to say about them.

Apart from his work as a missionary, Ryerson's methods of helping the Indians were similar to those used by present-day CUSO volunteers. What is CUSO? Find out what its members do, and where

They were not always at loggerheads, though. On the return trip, the men who had muttered were in charge of the ship. The weather was good and they amused themselves on deck. One of them was trying out a tune on the fife, not very successfully. Ryerson asked him for the fife and played the tune. The traders gathered around and listened, delighted and astonished. "From that hour they were my warm friends," remarked Ryerson with amusement.

During the years to come, many people were to comment on Ryerson's engaging personality. Certainly, his unforced charm and natural friendliness made it easy for him to get along with men and women from all walks of life.

In this first year of his mission, however, Ryerson was not particularly concerned with making friends. He had just made a powerful enemy.

An Ojibway family

"A Methodist Chapter 3
Preacher"

Egerton Ryerson's adversary was the Reverend Dr. John Strachan, Rector of York. Born in Scotland and raised a Presbyterian, he had come to Canada in 1799. Shortly afterwards, he joined the Anglican Church. A man of outstanding abilities, he was intelligent, sincere, brave, dedicated—and ambitious. (In 1827 he was to become Archdeacon of York and in 1839, Bishop.) He loved power, above all political power, and was influential in government circles. His influence was the result not only of his position and his personality, but grew naturally from a successful career as a teacher. Many members of the group surrounding the lieutenant-governor, which was already becoming known as the Family Compact, were his old students. This was the formidable man who was defied by an obscure 23-year-old Methodist preacher, 25 years his junior.

Strachan would probably have done even better in politics than in the church. Cardinal Richelieu is one example of a similar kind of cleric. Find out more about Richelieu's life. Do you know of any other churchmen who were politicians rather than priests?

In the summer of 1825, Bishop Mountain, Anglican Bishop of both Upper Canada (Ontario) and Lower Canada, had died. On the Sunday after his death, Strachan had preached the customary eulogy in his church at York. Instead of keeping to the point— praising the dead man—the Rector chose to use the occasion to attack some of the non-Anglican denominations, principally the Methodists. He accused them of being poorly educated and irresponsible. They were a menace to the province and also—rather inconsistently—inadequate. "What can fifty-three clergymen do, scattered over a country of greater extent than Great Britain?" he said. He went further: he branded them as Americans and, consequently, traitors to Upper Canada. This sermon was printed in the spring of 1826.

The Methodists (and other nonconformists) had always been discriminated against. Their church was not allowed to own land for churches, parsonages or

What is a nonconformist? What is the difference, if any, between a nonconformist and a Protestant?

THE BISHOP OF TORONTO.

John Strachan, when Bishop of Toronto

The famous grammar school in Cornwall, founded by Strachan in 1803, where he taught until 1812

cemeteries. Baptisms and marriages performed by their ministers were not legal. A greater grievance was that they were kept from benefiting from the Clergy Reserves, land that had been set aside to provide an income for Protestant clergymen. The trouble was that Strachan and other members of the Family Compact considered the Anglican Church to be the only Protestant denomination. Naturally, the other Protestant denominations loathed this injustice. The Methodists, as determined as any to get the share they felt their due, were against state support for their ministers. They wanted the money for education.

A leading Methodist obtained a copy of Strachan's sermon and read parts of it at the next monthly meeting in York. It caused an outburst of indignation. The accusation of treachery was the last straw; for those of Loyalist stock, it was the supreme insult. They had proved their devotion to their new country years before, in the War of 1812, many with their lives. All present at the meeting agreed that somebody must reply. Ryerson and his senior on the circuit, James Richardson, were chosen to write a rebuttal before the next meeting.

When the time came, Mr. Richardson had nothing to show, but Ryerson produced a long manuscript which he had written in the intervals of eight days' work, when he had ridden 100 miles and preached seven sermons. His colleagues insisted that he should read his letter, which he reluctantly did. It was received with so much enthusiasm — and sometimes with laughter — that there was only one opinion: it must be printed. Ryerson objected and tried to throw his paper in the fire; so one of his friends grabbed him, and another saved the precious manuscript. When Ryerson saw that they meant what they said, he gave in, only asking that he should be allowed to revise it. He was given permission and then returned to his circuit.

William Lyon Mackenzie had a long and stormy career as a journalist and politician in Upper Canada. Find out more about his activities and views

There was no difficulty in finding a publisher. Another Scot, a wild Highlander named William Lyon Mackenzie, had been sniping at Strachan for some two years. He was the founder and editor of a newspaper, *The Colonial Advocate,* in which he aired his violently anti-Family Compact views. Mackenzie had an affinity with everything anti-Establishment, and had already heard and written approvingly about Ryerson's sermons in York. He was therefore only too delighted to devote almost a whole issue of his paper to the young man's first blast at Strachan.

When the "Review of a Sermon, Preached by the Honourable and Reverend John Strachan . . . " was printed under the pseudonym of "A Methodist Preacher" it created an uproar. On the June evening when the newspaper was published, groups of excited people stood in front of their houses in York reading and discussing the article. Ryerson had not pulled his punches. In reply to Strachan's accusation of disloyalty, he wrote:

"John Strachan worries about republican principles instilled in [the] minds of people by religious teachers of other denominations. But they do not talk about politics as the Doctor does. They have something else to do . . . prayer and ministry of the word."

As to the inadequacy of 53 Methodist ministers in so large a country, he continued:

"For the Doctor's reflection and encouragement I would ask, What did twelve apostles do in the midst of an obstinate, barbarous and persecuting world?"

He also said in the plainest language that Strachan was

more interested in church money than in church teachings.

The intellectual excellence and force of "The Review" astonished Anglicans and Methodists. To the Anglicans, it must have seemed that the canary had eaten the cat; to the Methodists that a heaven-sent spokesman had emerged from their ranks. They were overwhelmed with joy and, like everyone else, wondered who "A Methodist Preacher" might be.

Ryerson published his first work under a pseudonym. Can you think of any other writers who did not always use their own names? Who were they, and what names did they choose?

One person had a special interest in the identity of the author. A few months after the "Preacher" had made his appearance, Ryerson went home on his first annual visit to his parents. For two days his father could talk of nothing except the battle royal that had developed. At last, while father and son were strolling in the orchard, Colonel Ryerson turned abruptly and said, "Egerton, they say that you are the author of these papers which are convulsing the whole country. I want to know whether you are or not."

Ryerson admitted that he was indeed the author.

"My God! we are all ruined!"

Fortunately, Colonel Ryerson lived to be 93, long enough to be proud of his famous son.

Curiously enough, the two people chiefly concerned were the last to hear of the commotion. Strachan had been in England and Ryerson on his travels. It was a disagreeable surprise for Strachan; and some letters hostile to the author appeared in the papers. This seriously disturbed Ryerson, who was not in the least prepared for the sensation he had caused. However, after thinking things over and praying for guidance: "I felt that I must either flee or fight. I decided upon the latter . . . and then went at my adversaries in good earnest."

And to good effect. Within four years, laws were passed to enable the nonconformist denominations to own land, and for the ministers to solemnize christenings and marriages. Progress had begun. The difficult question of the Clergy Reserves was not settled until 1854 when the land was sold by the government. With the exception of a reserve fund to cover annuities already granted to some Anglican clergymen, the rest of the money was given to the municipalities, mostly for education.

Chapter 4 **Journalist**

Ryerson had not been too busy to fall in love. In 1824 he was already thinking of marriage and of "The comforts and tranquillity of domestic happiness."

He had first met Hannah Aikman in 1821 when he went to lodge in her father's house while studying with Mr. Law at Hamilton. She was then seventeen years old and had been converted to Methodism the year before. She was also beautiful. It was not until 1824, however, that she and Ryerson became serious about each other. "Her fondness for me was extravagant," he wrote.

They became engaged but their prospects of marriage were poor. Ryerson had no money and no job. When he became a travelling preacher the following year, things looked rather worse. Hannah offered to release him from the engagement if he thought their marriage would make him less useful to the church. They then agreed that they would wait for three or four years.

Certainly, during this waiting period Ryerson wondered whether a man in his position should marry. Possibly Hannah had her doubts too, or perhaps her handsome boy friend took too long to make up his mind. Whatever the reason, for a short time she was engaged to his youngest brother Edwy. Exactly what happened is not known, but at the end of January, 1828, Ryerson received a stinging rebuke from his brother John: "The instability and indecision of character that you have manifested in this affare have not a little surprised me. . . ."

Hannah Aikman and Egerton Ryerson were married the following September. They had two children: John William, born in 1829, and Lucilla, three years younger.

Edwy Ryerson

Not long before his marriage, Ryerson had been transferred to Cobourg. He returned to York sooner than he had expected. In 1828, the Canadian Methodists separated from the American "connexion" and became the independent Methodist Episcopal

Egerton Ryerson: the young minister

Church in Canada. At the same time, the American church repaid them a proportion of the money they had contributed.

During their next conference, in 1829, the York Methodists decided to use this money to start their own weekly newspaper, to be called the *Christian Guardian*. Ryerson was elected editor. He was given $700 and told to go to New York to buy a printing press and whatever else was necessary. This was a tall order for someone who knew nothing about printing, but the Methodist Book Concern in New York gave him advice and help.

Although an assistant editor had also been elected, Ryerson wrote and got out the paper. The difficulties of doing this, "without a clerk, in the midst of our poverty, can hardly be realized," he said. The first number appeared on November 22, 1829 and sold about 500 copies.

The *Guardian's* main emphasis was on religion, good government and education, but Ryerson did not use it merely as a means of airing the Methodist views

An early printing press used by the Methodist publishing enterprise

The press illustrated in this chapter was a good one for its time. Find out something about modern printing. How has this book been printed?

on these burning topics. It is true that his articles were eagerly read and discussed, but he gave the newspaper a family slant. It contained Canadian and foreign news; a correspondence column; a parliamentary report; poetry; stories of pious lives; advice on farming and gardening; tips on health and household matters; and an advertising section.

Ryerson encouraged contributors. In issue Number 13, of March 13, 1830, an article on "Influence of Education (By a Young Lady)" appeared on the front page. Inside was a notice very gratifying to the editor: "Several articles intended for this day's paper are excluded for want of room."

In a time when religion was not kept in the closet during the week and brought out only on Sundays, and with Ryerson's talent and industry, the *Guardian* was bound to succeed. Soon the lieutenant-governor (who presumably took the official *Upper Canada Gazette*) was saying that it was the most widely read paper in the province. At the end of three years, circulation had increased to nearly 3,000.

For obvious reasons, the early issues carried the following notice:

"BOOKS, PAMPHLETS AND JOB WORK Executed at this Office with neatness and despatch, and on the most reasonable terms."

Write a short letter to the editor of the Christian Guardian *on any topic you think was important in 1829*

Part of the front page of an early issue of the Christian Guardian

CHRISTIAN GUARDIAN.

PUBLISHED FOR THE METHODIST EPISCOPAL CHURCH IN CANADA. E. RYERSON & F. METCALF, EDITORS.

VOL. I.   **YORK, SATURDAY, MARCH 13, 1830.**   **NO. 17.**

GUARDIAN OFFICE,

March-street, north of the New Court-House.

W. J. COATES, PRINTER.

TERMS.—THE CHRISTIAN GUARDIAN is published weekly, on Saturdays, at *twelve shillings and six pence*, a year, if paid in advance; or *fifteen shillings*, if paid in six months; or *seventeen shillings and six pence*, if not paid before the end of the year; *exclusive of postage.* Subscriptions paid within one month after receiving the first number will be considered in advance.

The Postage is four shillings a year; and must also be paid within one month after receiving the first number by those who wish to be considered as paying in advance.

All travelling and local Preachers of the M. E. Church are authorised Agents to procure Subscribers and forward their names with subscriptions: and to all authorized Agents who shall procure *fifteen* responsible subscribers, and aid in the collection, &c. one copy will be sent gratis.—The accounts will be kept with the subscribers individually, who alone will be held responsible.

No subscription will be received for less than six months: and no subscriber has a right to discontinue, except at our option, until all arrears are paid. Agents will be careful to attend to this.

The following unpretending and pleasant verses, were written on the occasion, of the Rice Lake Indians leaving their bark wigwams, on an Island in the Lake, and removing to their houses, where they intend to exchange the uncertain game of the chase, for the more sure supplies of industry and agriculture.—ED.

For the Christian Guardian.

WIGKEWAUM * FAREWELL.

Po-mah Pam-dusk-koo-do-yongk † I see,
A house by Christians made for me.
Jesus does this and all things well;
Smoky bark wigkewaum, farewell.

The Indian tribes long time before
I ever wandered on this shore,
Lov'd better much the warhoop yell,
Than saying, wigkewaum, farewell

In vain the white man tried to tame,
The red man's heart, 'twas still the same;
'Till one came who of Jesus tell;
I then say, bark wigkewaum, farewell.

My tomahawk away I throw;
My moog-koo-mon † I need not now;

confined to a *few*, and the advantages which education affords, not being enjoyed, *numbers* doubtless, are doomed to blush unseen, and sink into oblivion, possessing genius and talents sufficient to render them capable of doing honour to themselves, their country, and the world. From these considerations we see at once the necessity of *some* means, in addition to those bestowed by nature, to call into operation the energies and faculties of the mind; to rouse to action the dormant spirits, and excite in the breast of the young aspirant, a spirit of active and laudable exertion in the pursuit of knowledge. And to effect this, the United States evidently appear to be among those which bid fair to vie with the most enlightened nations of the earth in the means afforded to facilitate the progress of science and literature, and to record her name on the pages of history as the nursery of science and virtue, and to hand down to posterity the glory of her literary achievements. As a proof of its powerful effects on a *community*, we may look at Great Britain and see the rapid advances which have been made not only in the commercial & political world, but in the arts and sciences; which have been carried to such

This was the germ of a new enterprise. By 1833, the Methodists took another big step forward. They decided to open a bookstore at the *Guardian* office, stocked with books imported from the United States and Britain. Ryerson was appointed book agent, and no Methodist preacher was allowed to order books for sale except through the book agent. From these small beginnings, first under the name of the Methodist Book Concern and then as The Ryerson Press, grew the largest printing and publishing house in Canada. In the 141 years of its existence, it exerted a strong influence on Canadian education and literature and became a part of Canada's cultural heritage.

Bliss Carman and Duncan Campbell Scott were two famous Canadian poets whose work was published by the Methodist Book Concern. Read some of their poetry. Do you see differences or similarities? Or both?

Ryerson's happy married life was short. Hannah Ryerson died early in 1832, two weeks after the birth of Lucilla. With this terrible exception, these were good years for Ryerson. He had matured quickly, and the young man who was reluctant to appear in print had disappeared long before. He was well on the way out when, in 1826, Ryerson had gone straight to the lieutenant-governor, Sir Peregrine Maitland, to report on the state of the Port Credit Indians.

The youthful Ryerson had originally gained a reputation for his preaching, although most people agreed that his brother William was the more gifted speaker. His experience at the *Guardian* had enabled him to blossom as a writer, and at this time it was as a writer that he was most valuable in fighting his church's battles. He was sorry that differences existed between Christians; he respected the teachings of the Anglican Church while hating the privilege it stood for. But once involved, he relished the thrust and parry of conflict.

In Ryerson's scale of values, preaching the Gospel was always his first duty. But he was also ambitious; he had acknowledged as much in his diary and counted it as a mark against himself. However, he could not help realizing that his talents fitted him for a different career from that of a circuit rider. His self-confidence grew with his reputation. Soon both were to be tested in different surroundings.

The Reverend James Evans, a friend and colleague of Ryerson, invented an alphabet, known as Cree syllabics, so that Indians and Eskimos could write their languages. He carved his type from bullets and the lead linings of old tea chests and bound some of his hymn books in deerskin

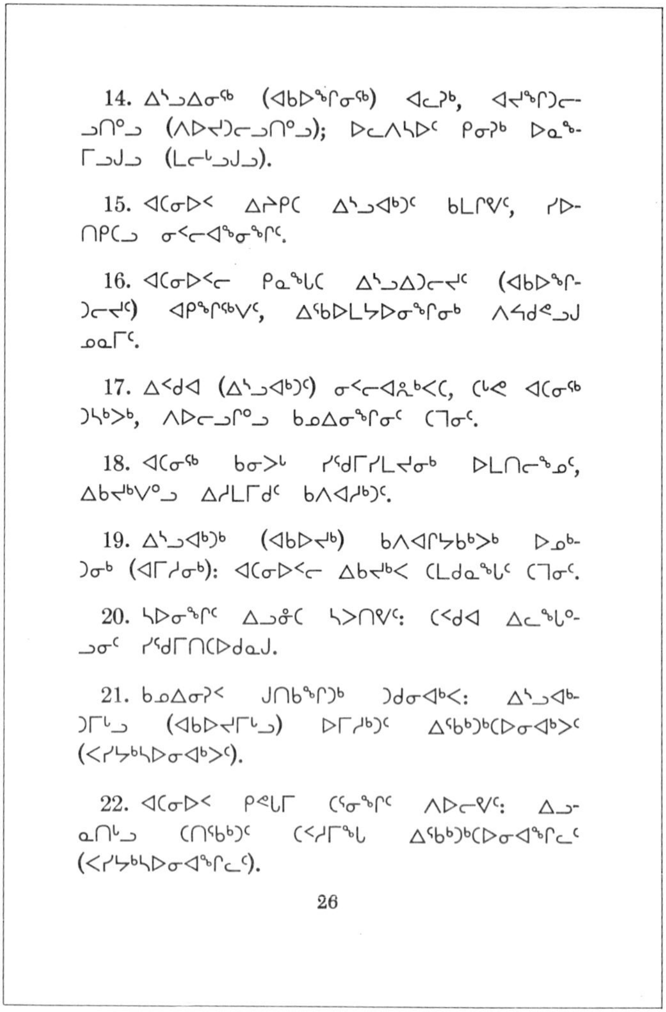

14. ᐃᔅᓗᐃᓂᖅ (ᐊᑲᐅᖏᓂᖅ) ᐊᓚᕈᒃ, ᐊᔪᖏᑐᓚ-
ᓗᑎᓪᓗ (ᐱᐅᔪᑐᓚᓗᑎᓪᓗ); ᐅᓚᐱᓴᐅᑦ ᑭᓂᕈᒃ ᐅᓇᖕ-
ᒥᓗᒍᓗ (ᒪᓚᓪᓗᒍᓗ).

15. ᐊᑕᓂᐅᑉ ᐃᓱᑭᑕ ᐃᔅᓗᐊᒃᑐᑦ ᑲᒪᒋᕐᐯᑦ, ᓯᐅ-
ᑎᑭᑕᓗ ᓂᑉᓚᐊᖕᓂᖏᑦ.

16. ᐊᑕᓂᐅᑉᓚ ᑭᓇᖕᒐᑕ ᐃᔅᓗᐃᑐᓚᔪᑦ (ᐊᑲᐅᖏ-
ᑐᓚᔪᑦ) ᐊᑭᖏᖅᐯᑦ, ᐃᖅᑲᐅᒪᔭᐅᓂᖏᓂᒃ ᐱᓭᑯᕝᓗᒍ
ᓄᓇᒥᑦ.

17. ᐃᑉᑯᐊ (ᐃᔅᓗᐊᒃᑐᑦ) ᓂᑉᓚᐊᖖᒃᐸᑕ, ᑕᓪᓓ ᐊᑕᓂᖅ
ᑐᓴᒃᐳᒃ, ᐱᐅᓚᓗᒥᓪᓗ ᑲᓄᐃᓂᖏᓂᑦ ᑕᒣᓂᑦ.

18. ᐊᑕᓂᖅ ᑲᓂᐳᓪ ᓯᖅᑯᒥᓯᒪᔪᓂᒃ ᐅᒪᑎᓚᖕᓄᑦ,
ᐃᑲᔪᒃᐯᓪᓗ ᐃᓱᒪᒥᑯᑦ ᑲᐱᐊᓱᒃᑐᑦ.

19. ᐃᔅᓗᐊᒃᑐᒃ (ᐊᑲᐅᔪᒃ) ᑲᐱᐊᒋᔭᒃᑲᒃᐳᒃ ᐅᓄᒃ-
ᑐᓂᒃ (ᐊᒥᓱᓂᒃ): ᐊᑕᓂᐅᑉᓚ ᐃᑲᔪᒃᐸ ᑕᒪᑯᓇᖕᒐᑦ ᑕᒣᓂᑦ.

20. ᓴᐅᓂᖏᑦ ᐃᓗᓃᑕ ᓴᐳᑎᕓᑦ: ᑕᑉᑯᐊ ᐃᓚᖕᒐᓪ-
ᓗᓂᑦ ᓯᖅᑯᒥᑎᑕᐅᑯᓇᒍ.

21. ᑲᓄᐃᓂᕈᑉ ᒍᑎᑲᖏᑐᒃ ᑐᑯᓂᐊᒃᐸ: ᐃᔅᓗᐊᒃ-
ᑐᒥᓪᓗ (ᐊᑲᐅᔪᒥᓪᓗ) ᐅᒥᓱᒃᑐᑦ ᐃᖅᑲᒃᑐᒃᑕᐅᓂᐊᒃᐳᑦ
(ᐸᓯᔭᒃᓴᐅᓂᐊᒃᐳᑦ).

22. ᐊᑕᓂᐅᑉ ᑭᓕᑲᒥ ᑕᖅᓂᖏᑦ ᐱᐅᓚᕓᑦ: ᐃᓗ-
ᓇᑎᓪᓗ ᑕᑎᖅᑲᒃᑐᑦ ᑕᑉᓱᒥᖕᒐ ᐃᖅᑲᒃᑐᒃᑕᐅᓂᐊᖏᓛᑦ
(ᐸᓯᔭᒃᓴᐅᓂᐊᖏᓛᑦ).

26

A page from an Eskimo prayer book, using Evans' syllabics, printed by The Ryerson Press 120 years later

Diplomat—and Undiplomatic

Chapter 5

Ryerson was going abroad on church business.

At this time, the Methodists in Upper Canada had to struggle not only with the Canadian Anglicans but also with the British Methodists. The Anglicans in Canada and the Methodists in Britain both believed that the Canadians were in danger of being dominated by the American Methodists. Rather than see this happen, the British preferred to do the dominating themselves, and tried their best to send missionaries to Canada. The Canadians strongly resisted. Naturally, they wanted to run their own church. In such a state of affairs, politics and religion became too closely interwoven to be separated. Egerton Ryerson was about to take his first step into this double world.

In 1832, he was chosen to go to England to negotiate what seemed to be the only possible solution: the union of the British and Canadian churches. This would give the British no excuse for infiltration, and the Canadians would profit by being entitled to financial help from the church in England. Ryerson was also given the tasks of petitioning the government on the subject of the Clergy Reserves, and trying to raise money to complete Upper Canada Academy, the non-denominational school for higher education which the Methodists had founded in Cobourg two years before.

He sailed from New York in March of 1833 and was horribly seasick. Although he was a brave and skilful sailor on his native lakes, the Atlantic always defeated him. (After a later crossing, he wrote to John: "I . . . was distinguished amongst the servants of the steamer as 'the sick gentleman'.") He went straight to London, where he had the exciting experience of preaching at Wesley's own chapel in City Road.

He found a little time for sightseeing. He visited the House of Commons twice but was disappointed. He

London, England, in the 1830s

Stonehenge has always been a mystery. Recently, researchers have come up with some interesting new ideas on the origin and purpose of Stonehenge, and have written several books on their conclusions. In your opinion, are the new theories convincing?

thought the proceedings lacked dignity. He went on tour, preaching at every stop and asking for money for the academy. Travelling to Exeter, he crossed Salisbury Plain, where the ancient Stonehenge is located. On the way to Nottingham, he passed through Sherwood Forest and thought for a moment of Robin Hood.

Back in London, he had two interviews with Edward Stanley, the Colonial Secretary, about the Clergy Reserves. Mr. Stanley was surprised to hear that most Canadian Methodist ministers were not "Yankees" controlled by the church in the States.

Another important contact was Joseph Hume, the Radical member of parliament who had been chosen by the Methodists in Canada to present their petition to the king. Hume was a friend of William Lyon Mackenzie, who was also in London at the time, and the three men met. Ryerson did not think Hume was a suitable person to champion the Canadian cause. He was an atheist, and had angered religious people in England by opposing a Bill to end slavery. He was neither the best man nor the best politician.

In the intervals of all the preaching and politicking, the union between the two churches was successfully concluded, although it did not last long. After five busy months, Ryerson was back in Canada as editor of the *Guardian*. His success would have been creditable to someone used to church and secular politics; for a young, inexperienced man, in totally strange surroundings, who had never seen a town larger than

York, it was a triumph. Perhaps, accustomed to his continual war with Strachan, he had found nothing in England to intimidate him.

Once home, Ryerson decided to marry again. Mary Armstrong had been a friend of Hannah Ryerson. She was affectionate, sensible and practical. "Truly I love her fervently . . . " They were married in the fall of 1833. Ryerson had a new wife and his children a second mother. John would not need a mother much longer; he died two years later, aged six.

Ryerson did not have to hunt for a subject that would interest his readers. He would write about his travels, and the first installment of "Impressions made by our late visit to England" appeared in the *Guardian*. It proved to be almost as big a bombshell as "the Review". In this first article, Ryerson described the English political parties as he saw them.

The two big British parties of the time were the Whigs (Liberals) and the Tories (Conservatives). The Radicals, or reformers, were the minority party. Ryerson thought little of all three parties. He divided the Tories into two kinds: the ultra-Tory, whom he called "a tyrant in politics, and a bigot in religion"; and the moderate Tory, who acted from religious motives. In his opinion, most English Methodists were moderate Tories. The Whigs he considered lightweights without principles, ready to sacrifice anything to stay in power. Lastly, he turned his guns on the smallest party—the Radicals. "Radicalism in England appeared to me to be but another word for Republicanism, with the name of King instead of President." He went on to say that some Radical editors in Canada had been "amongst the lowest of the English radicals" before emigrating.

It would have taken less than this to bring Mackenzie, until now Ryerson's ally, screaming at his heels. Abuse was his strong suit. On the evening of the day that Ryerson's article was published, he let fly in *The Colonial Advocate:*

"The *Christian Guardian,* under the management of Egerton Ryerson, has gone over to the enemy, — press, types and all — and hoisted the colours of a cruel, vindictive Tory priesthood. . . . "

Most serious of all, the Methodists themselves

William Lyon Mackenzie

Write a nose-to-nose dialogue between Colonel Joseph Ryerson and William Lyon Mackenzie

began to doubt Ryerson's good faith, when he described English Methodists as even moderate Tories. They became insecure and bitter; the union lost some of its bloom; the circulation of the *Guardian* dropped. Ryerson had published his views in entire sincerity but without sufficient thought of the consequences. It proved a colossal blunder. For some years, he was one of the most unpopular men in the province. The damage to his reputation persisted for a long time.

The section on English politics was never finished. Two later articles dealt with religious matters. In any case, the space was needed for the arguments. On the credit side, Ryerson did a service to Upper Canadians by sounding the alarm against the Radicals. As John Ryerson told his brother, "You can see plainly that it is not Reform, but Revolution they are after." When Mackenzie's rebellion came in 1837, what might have been a serious insurrection fizzled out.

King Street, Toronto, in the 1830s

Ryerson and Strachan continued to fight the good fight but became almost dear enemies. In 1838, Ryerson sent the Archdeacon a copy of his sermon on the rebellion and received a gracious acknowledgement. When Strachan's church was destroyed by fire the following year, Ryerson offered him the use of one of the Methodist churches. This time, Strachan wrote a genuinely warm and grateful reply. Then, in 1842, it happened: the two met.

The extraordinary thing was that it had not occurred before. Undoubtedly, one reason was that Strachan and Ryerson moved in different social circles. This time, though, they were well and truly brought together—in a stage coach travelling from Toronto to Kingston (York had become the city of Toronto in 1834).

Ryerson described the encounter: "For the first time in my life I found myself in company with the Lord Bishop of Toronto, my legs locked in with his Lordship's. . . . Conversation took place on several important topics, on scarcely any of which did I see reason to differ from the Bishop." Nor could he, since Strachan expressed some handsome opinions on subjects that Ryerson had been fighting for for years.

All in all, he found the great man exceedingly pleasant. By 1842, times had changed: the Methodists could no longer be ignored. Ryerson was on the way to becoming a great man himself.

Ryerson printed this in 1842. In his autobiography, published in 1883 after his death, the editor left out the words "and my legs locked in with his Lordship's." This is an example of the growth of prudery in the 1800s. Legs were called "limbs" in polite society. Find other similar examples

GUARDIAN.

:E OF THE WESLEYAN-METHODIST CHURCH IN CANADA.

.Y, DECEMBER 13, 1837.   WHOLE No. 422.

THE GUARDIAN.

WEDNESDAY, *December* 13, 1837.

As a considerable portion of our last week's papers fell into the hands of Mackenzie, when robbing the mails, we have re-inserted in this number some communications and intelligence which we thought would be interesting to our readers.

Tuesday Morning, Dec. 5.
REBELLION IN THE HOME DIS-
TRICT!—TORONTO IN ARMS!!

Little did we think that it would be our painful duty to state that Mazkenzie's measures were so far ripened into revolution as to lead already to armed opposition to the constituted authorities.

THIS IS THE FACT. An armed force is collected on Yonge-street, and is threatening an attack upon the City. The Governor, like a brave representative of his youthful Queen, is under arms at the head of several hundreds of loyal men. The streets are being barricaded. The garrison and the market buildings are placed in the best possible state of defence that the short notice would admit. Unless Divine Providence interfere,much blood will be shed. *Canadians of every class ! Canadian* REFORMERS! are you prepared to shed the blood of your country-men ? Can any thing Mackenzie can offer you compensate for the guilt you must incur if you enrol under his revolutionary banner, and *deluge your fruitful fields with blood ?* For God's sake pause ! Frown

Yesterday the dwelling house of Dr. Horne was burned to ashes, and several others plundered.

Last night, about eight o'clock, a piquet guard of 32 men, under Sheriff Jarvis, was suddenly attacked by a large party of rifle-men, who opened upon them a smart fire, but happsly without effect. It was briskly returned by the little band with more fatal precision. One of the assailants was left dead, and it is said that two others were carried off by the insurgents, mortally wounded.

Yesterday morning His Excellency humanely requested Drs. Rolph and Baldwin to visit the head quarters of the rebels, and to urge them in the name of humanity to desist from their wicked designs, and to return peaceably to their families, and thus prevent the effusion of blood. We understand that the appeal of His Excellency was touching and eloquent ; but it was in vain. Mackenzie, who has now ventured his all, dictated terms which no Governor could assent to without forfeiting his honour and his head.]

Wednesday, Dec. 13.
TOTAL DEFEAT OF THE REBELS!

Last week we gave a statement of the commencement of the insurrection in this District, and its progress up to Wednesday morning ; which is republished above. During Wednesday large numbers of loyal volunteers were constantly coming in, and most vigorous measures were adopted for the defence of the city, and for the dispersion of the rebels. The state of public feeling was roused to the highest pitch of indignation on learning that Mackenzie and a band of desperadoes had stopped the mails, and *robbed* the bags and the passengers of all the money on which they could lay their hands ! as also on learning from various prisoners that were brought in that his plan was to fire the City in various quarters, by force or stealth, and thus reduce it to ashes, and its inhabitants to destitution. All the fire companies were held in readiness, strong patroles paraded all the streets, picquet guards were posted at the various avenues leading to the City; the Bank, the market and parliament buildings, and the garrison were placed

of men were immediately marched out, who dispersed them after killing one of them. The bridge was saved ; but the buildings, which were the property of the widow of the late S. Washburn, Esq., were entirely destroyed.

The Artillery companies were commanded by Captains Leckie and Stennett. The Cavalry by Dr. Widmer. The chief command devolved on that experienced and highly-respected officer, Col. Fitzgibbon. The cool and steady courage with which the militia went into action has been the subject of laudatory remark by many who have seen severe service. It would be invidious to make any distinction in noticing the bravery of the volunteer companies. All have done nobly, and have earned the lasting gratitude of their country.

The rebel force, before the action was variously estimated by their partizans at from 1000 to 1400 ; but since the defeat they report it as having been only from 500 to 600. The volunteer force which marched against them was about 1500 strong. The loss on the part of Mackenzie's dupes is supposed to be 11 killed, (7 have been positively ascertained,) and 14 wounded ; some of them, as we know, dangerously. On the part of the volunteers, only three wounded, all slightly, and no loss of life.

It is with indescribable emotions of mingled sorrow and joy, that we review the progress of affairs during the past eventful week. Sorrow, that any portion of our fellow-countrymen should have allowed themselves to be so duped by a few unprincipled and ambitious men, as to take up offensive weapons against a paternal government, and against the liberties and lives of their unoffending neighbours. Joy, that their nefarious designs, so far as concerns this City and its vicinity, have been in so remarkable a manner developed and counteracted.

In no instance, perhaps, has the interposition of Divine Providence been more strongly marked than in the deliverance of this city, from one of the most diabolical, and cruel plots which ever stained the page of history. Few persons, how-

The Guardian *of December 13, 1837 reports Mackenzie's rebellion*

Victoria College

Chapter 6

Education, and in particular Upper Canada Academy, became more and more important to Ryerson, until he was completely involved with it.

His first fund-raising visit to England had been followed by another, two years later. Although finances were desperate and the academy still not open, this time he went to ask for a charter of incorporation from the king, and a government grant. The Anglican King's College enjoyed both, although it was still only on paper. The Methodists, poor as they were, had managed to raise sufficient money among themselves to build a beautiful college, already almost finished. They too were determined to have a charter and a grant. Ryerson's instructions were to *"Beg, beg, beg,"* and he did just that. He wrote letters to many prominent people or visited them asking for contributions. He reached more humble folk through his sermons.

He found begging "a wearisome business." So were the negotiations with the government. There was nothing for it but to wait while the wheels of the Colonial Office began to turn. Although his wife was with him, and their daughter Sophia was born in London, Ryerson was homesick for Canada, "my dear native land." He did well. By beating a path to the Colonial Office door, by endless letters and statements, in which he argued his case with the assurance of an experienced lawyer, he received the royal charter and a grant of $8,000 a year—half the amount he had asked for. After an exile of more than eighteen months, Ryerson and his family were able to go home.

Meanwhile, two months before his return, on June 18, 1836, Upper Canada Academy was opened to men and women students. The occasion was marked by an impressive ceremony, with a procession in which

While in England, one person Ryerson wrote to for a donation to Upper Canada Academy was the Bishop of London. He refused because the scheme had not been approved by the bishop of the diocese. Write a polite letter explaining the situation and again asking for money

Cobourg in 1841

Choose two subjects, topical in 1836-41, for the Upper Canada Academy debating society: one that the principal would approve; one that he would not

ministers, members of the committee, the first principal, the Reverend Matthew Richey, the architect and the students all took part. It was a great day for the village of Cobourg; a great day for Canada.

In spite of teething troubles and continual money worries (the British government was slow in paying its share), the academy flourished. Founded as a "literary and religious Institution," it was remarkably liberal for its time. (The progressive attitude, however, did not extend to the students' debating society; subjects to be debated had first to be approved by the principal.) The curriculum included Latin, Greek, mathematics, oratory and astronomy. At the first annual public examination in 1837, the women did better than the men in astronomy. "The young ladies" also had drawing lessons.

In 1841, Upper Canada Academy became a university and changed its name to Victoria College. In September of that year, Ryerson was invited to become the new university's first principal. He believed that the ideals of religion and education were inseparable, and accepted the post. In October he came to Cobourg to explain to the staff and students his ideas about the function of the college.

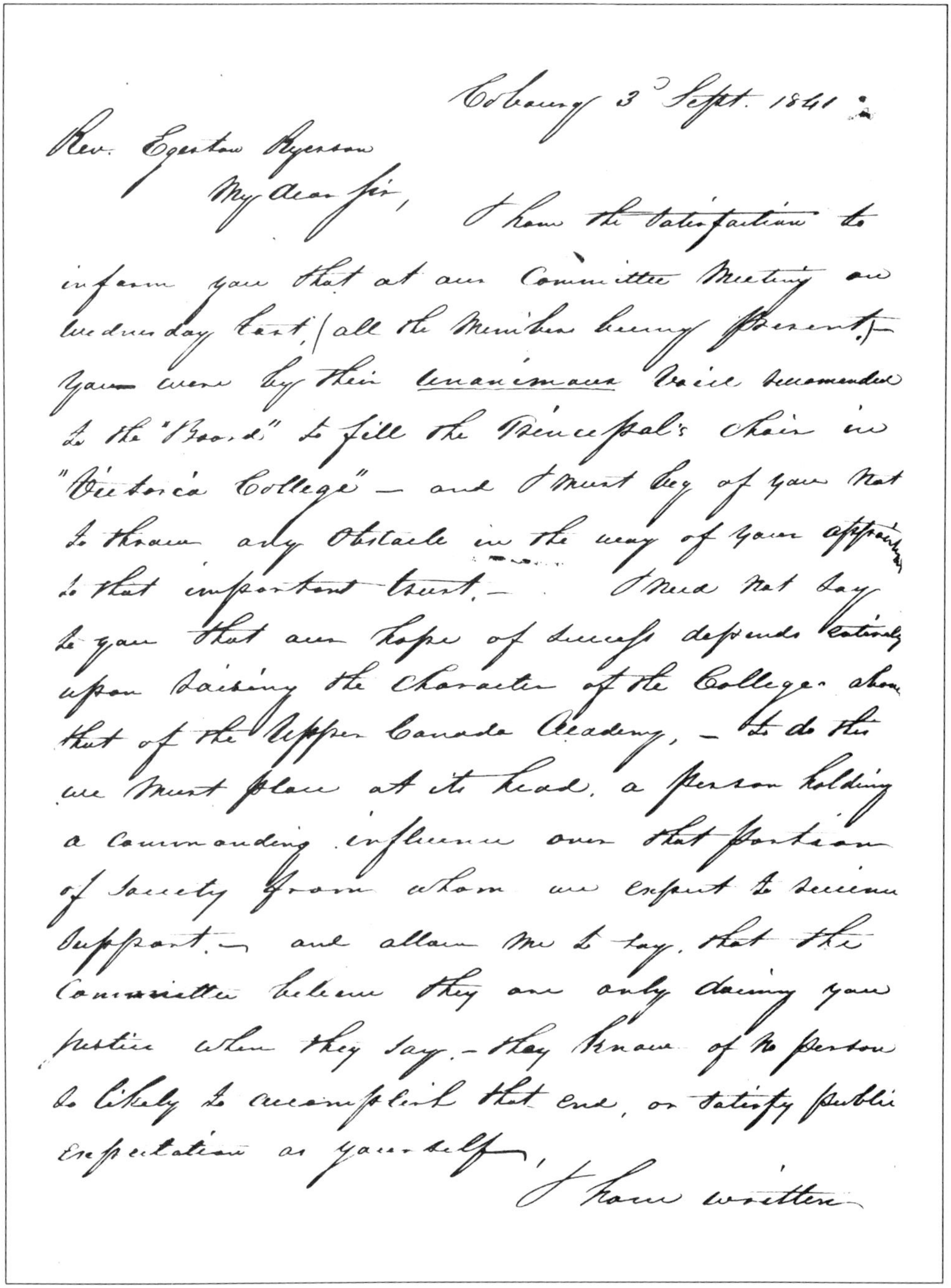

Cobourg 3 Sept. 1841

Rev. Egerton Ryerson

My dear Sir,

I have the satisfaction to inform you that at our Committee Meeting on Wednesday last, (all the Members being present,) you were by their *unanimous* voice recommended to the "Board" to fill the Principal's chair in "Victoria College" — and I must beg of you not to throw any obstacle in the way of your appointment to that important trust. — I need not say to you that our hope of success depends entirely upon raising the Character of the College above that of the Upper Canada Academy, — to do this we must place at its head, a person holding a commanding influence over that portion of society from whom we expect to receive support. — and allow me to say, that the Committee believe they are only doing you justice when they say. — they know of no person so likely to accomplish that end, or satisfy public expectation as yourself, —

I have written

Ryerson's letter of appointment as principal of Victoria College

Write a report on the modern educational system, stating your ideas about the purpose of education

Ryerson was, above all, practical. In his speech, he stressed the need for education to be useful. To be useful, it must be suited to the future lives of the students. That is, it had to be Canadian. To adopt, second-hand, the entire educational system of another country would be futile. Furthermore, to build good citizens, education had to be Christian in the widest sense, not limited to a single denomination. (At least one of the staff was a Presbyterian, and among his audience were members of nearly every Christian community in the province.)

One of education's main tasks, he continued, was to make students hard-working. Few had ever achieved anything except by hard work. This meant self-discipline: getting up early; not wasting time; persevering even when discouraged. No one could accuse Ryerson of not practising what he preached.

Do you agree with Ryerson's statement that little can be achieved except by hard work? Justify your position

Owing to other engagements in Toronto, Ryerson was unable to move to Victoria until June of 1842, when he was formally inaugurated as principal, and handed the keys of the college. In his first speech as head of the university, he emphasized the value of an education in English although, he said, he did not underrate the classics. This was a knock at Strachan's British tradition of education only in Greek and Latin.

The new principal announced that the science department was to be enlarged to include chemistry, mineralogy and geology, and that two new departments — philosophy and rhetoric — were to be set up. (Later, French and German were added.) He also commented on the need to avoid specialization, and to achieve a balance between arts and science that would be reflected in the balanced character of the student.

In Ryerson, Victoria College got exactly what it needed: a first-rate teacher and an outstanding administrator. He had never spared himself and saw no reason to spare others. As a teacher, he was strict and often demanded too much from average students. The bright ones thrived. (One student who suffered at first under the new regime was Ryerson's nephew Egerton, John's son.) His rules were tough: vacations were interruptions and sources of "trouble" so they were abolished, except on Christmas and New Year's Days.

Victoria College, Cobourg

*Victoria University, Toronto. It
moved from Cobourg in 1892*

But Ryerson was more than a disciplinarian; he could also be a friend to his pupils. One of his most gifted students saw this side of him. He wrote an account of his first evening as a freshman at Victoria. Ryerson visited him in his room:

"I shall never forget that interview. He took me by the hand; and few men could express as much by a mere hand-shake as he. . . . His manner was so gracious and paternal—his sympathy so quick and genuine—his counsel so ready and cheering . . . that not only was my heart *his* from that hour, but my future career seemed brighter and more certain than it had ever appeared before."

From the time Ryerson came into residence, women students vanished. He was ahead of his time in his strong views on the advantages of a good education for his own daughters, and for all women. But he felt equally strongly that women must be educated separately. There must be no danger of their "distracting" the men from their studies. Women did not return to Victoria College for thirty-six years.

During his first year at Cobourg, Ryerson was awarded the honorary degree of Doctor of Divinity by the Wesleyan University at Middletown, Connecticut. Eighteen forty-two was a good year: a new career, recognition and, in September, the birth of a son, also named John. The life of the second John was brief; he died after six months.

Ryerson was at Victoria for only two years. During that time he set his mark upon the college and saw it through a period of adjustment. He had met a new challenge more than adequately. This experience, however, was merely a prelude to the work for which he will always be remembered.

Architect Chapter 7

In 1844, Egerton Ryerson was appointed Chief Superintendent of Common Schools for Canada West*. Two
years later he was promoted to Chief Superintendent
of Education, a post he held until his retirement thirty
years later. The new Education Office was not a
government department and the superintendent was
responsible only to the governor-general.

*In 1841, the Act of Union
created the United Province of
Canada. Lower Canada became
Canada East and Upper Canada,
Canada West

To be independent of party politics was an
inestimable advantage. As Ryerson put it: " . . . I knew
no other party than that of the country at large. . . . "
Naturally, he had to work through the machinery of
government, chiefly with two ministers: the provincial
secretary, to whom he sent his reports, and the
attorney-general who steered the necessary Bills
through the Legislature.

When Ryerson came to the Education Office at the
age of 41, he was in the prime of life and at the height
of his powers. His personality, his talents, and his
experience all fitted him for a position which, in turn,
gave him the scope and responsibility that his nature
demanded. The right man was in the right place.

*John, William, and Egerton
Ryerson*

John Ryerson, who was not the type to be blinded by their relationship, said bluntly that the post had been created for his brother. He declared that Egerton was better qualified for the job than any other person in the province, and that, as superintendent, " . . . you can be of more service to the Church, and the country generally, than in any other way." Ryerson considered the work " . . . the most splendid field of usefulness that could engage the energies of man . . . "

In the early days of the century, schools appeared almost by chance. Some were established wherever there was someone able or at least willing to teach. Others were private or church schools for children whose parents could afford to pay fees, either in money or kind. ("For each boy *eight guineas* per annum and one cord of wood" were the fees for one of the first schools in York.) Even these privileged students had little chance of obtaining a good education because of the poor calibre of the teachers. A Strachan, a James Mitchell, were rare. The majority of schoolmasters were ignorant, even illiterate, and had graduated in one subject only—strapping. Not the least of Ryerson's intentions was to educate teachers.

This sketch of a common school was drawn by an inspector in December, 1845. He called his picture the "March of Intellect"

Gradually, the government began legislating for schools: first, for grammar schools, which were for fee-paying students; then for common schools, many in the rural areas. Any parish that could produce a minimum of twenty students was entitled to a small grant, the parents providing the buildings. These were unhappy places, primitive log cabins, where in winter students froze and in summer they suffocated. There was little or no equipment. Pupils sat on backless benches, wrote on slates, and — if they were lucky — practised writing with quill pens.

The few books, supplied by the students themselves, were often those used by parents in their own schooldays. Other books, brought into the country by American teachers, were anti-British and therefore anti-Canadian. The chief method of teaching was to get pupils to learn stock answers by heart and repeat them parrot-fashion. Even so, only about half the number of students of school age ever went to school. Of the rest, some went for a year at most, or were taken away as soon as they grew strong enough to help on the farm.

The Chief Superintendent of Education

The task ahead was immense, and Ryerson had to start from scratch. His aims were to "stud" the country with suitable schools and supply them with teachers and books; to raise "a wretched employment [teaching] to an honourable profession"; to create libraries in every township; to develop everywhere "latent intellect, the most precious wealth of the country"; and to see, "at no distant day, every child of my native land in the school-going way." He intended to achieve one system of education " . . . from the a, b, c, of the child, up to the matriculation of the youth into the Provincial University. . . . " Ryerson was able to achieve much of this by his School Acts of 1846, 1850 and 1871.

The first thing Ryerson did after his appointment was to see for himself what was happening in education and welfare in the countries of Europe. In fact, he had made it a condition of his acceptance that he should be given a year's leave of absence without pay for this purpose. He left for Europe in late October, 1844 and before he returned to Canada had visited the United Kingdom, Belgium, Holland, France,

Bavaria and other German states—including Prussia—Austria, Switzerland and Italy.

The snobbery of the English educational system was distasteful to Ryerson. Leaving England for Holland, at The Hague he was very impressed by a free school of 800 poor children from eight to twelve years of age, who were supplied with books and stationery (and prayers four times a day)—"rod never used." In Haarlem, a few days later, he talked to a man whose business for 40 years had been to "make school-masters." At Amsterdam, he had an interview with the government inspector of schools. While at Brussels, in Belgium, he managed to fit in a trip to the battlefield of Waterloo, where he stayed three hours. Then on to Ghent, where he visited a prison and a poorhouse which housed about 300 poor old people.

Ryerson stayed for two months in Paris. This was an important part of his tour. While principal of Victoria College, he had begun to learn Hebrew; now he intended to master French. He did this not only because French was specially necessary in Canada, but also because the study of this language was part of the education of every cultured person.

It was hard going and at first he was discouraged, but by the end of two months he was able to speak French fluently. As well as having private lessons, he attended lectures at the university on a wide variety of subjects. At first he was lost, but not for long. Ryerson's diary records his progress. Soon after his arrival the laconic entry reads: " . . . heard lecture on history." A month later, the titles flower into "Histoire de Littérature Grecque," "Théologie Morale," and "Éloquence latine." He was on his way.

Small, narrow-minded Toronto was far over the horizon, so he spent an ecumenical Sunday attending three services in one day: at the Wesleyan chapel, the Anglican church, and the Roman Catholic Church of the Madeleine, "most magnificent." Of course he went to the Chamber of Deputies, and visited the other places that tourists in Paris still do—and said much the same things about them. Towards the end of his stay he visited several Protestant schools, including a Normal School (teachers' training college) for women, which had two Model Schools, one for boys and one

The Reverend Dr. Thomas Arnold, headmaster of Rugby School in England from 1828 to 1842, transformed not only Rugby but the whole English public school (boarding school) system for generations. Read something about Dr. Arnold's life and ideas

What famous battle occurred at Waterloo?

for girls, where the nineteen student teachers could practise teaching.

After leaving France, Ryerson went south to Italy. At Naples he dutifully climbed Vesuvius, whose crater was spouting lava all around; but the highlights of his visit were two long talks. One was with the Jesuit Prefect of Educational Institutions, the other with a priest from the United States, both of whom gave him much useful information.

The fact that Ryerson visited Prussia twice, at the beginning and end of his trip, speaks for itself. He was much taken with the system that he found there. In Berlin, in September of 1845, he saw "the great schools of this magnificent city . . . embracing both classical and scientific departments." He inspected the City Trade School and, in nearby Potsdam, visited the Normal School: "witnessed the teaching of two of the pupil-teachers, — both used the blackboard, and both appeared thorough masters of what they were teaching, using no books, — other pupil-teachers were looking on; never saw a finer class of young men." He finished the tour by going to Scotland and Ireland. With his mind full of all these experiences, Ryerson arrived home in December, 1845.

On his return, he wrote his classic report on a "System of Public Instruction for Upper Canada," in which he adapted the best of what he had seen for the use of Canadians. It contained proposals for a far wider course of studies than the "three Rs". History, geography, nature study, and Ryerson's own love, music, were necessary to feed students' minds. With memories of the beautiful works of art he had seen abroad, Ryerson asked for reproductions of famous paintings and statues to be placed in schoolrooms. He also recommended the formation of libraries and stated that the establishment of Normal Schools was absolutely essential.

In the report, Ryerson restated his belief that the purpose of education was not to cram students with knowledge but to fit them for life, "as Christians, as persons in business, and also as members of the civil community in which they live." He then drafted the Bill which would put the report into effect. This resulted in the Common School Act of 1846 which drew the first outline of the great plan that Ryerson was formulating at the time.

The Act of 1846 established a central provincial authority responsible for education. This was the General Board of Education whose seven members were appointed by the governor-general. The Superintendent of Education, Ryerson, was one; the other six toed the Ryerson line. The board controlled courses of study, textbooks, teacher training, and the newly formed system of inspectors. Not all authority was centralized; provision was made for local district superintendents supervising several school "sections."

The most important principle of the Act was that of free education for all. Not everyone was willing to pay taxes for schools, and acceptance came about only gradually. To Ryerson, payment from taxes was the foundation of a system of public education, but he was prepared for objections and foresaw that they would come chiefly from the rich. He told the story of a Methodist magistrate who had said that he did not wish to be "compelled to educate *all the brats* in the neighbourhood." Ryerson replied that the law was meant to "compel *selfish* rich men to do what they ought to do" but would not of their own accord.

Design a poster advocating free education for all. Think of some good slogans to help your cause

Ryerson's solution to the problem of getting people to accept the idea of free schools was simple: he would tell them about it himself. In the fall of 1847, he set out on a two-month tour of 21 districts. His name was now known throughout the province, so before leaving he sent an announcement to be inserted in all the local papers that he would give a lecture entitled "The Importance of Education to an Agricultural, a Manufacturing, and a Free People." The next morning, at each place, he met the district school superintendent, clergymen, councillors, school trustees, teachers and all local people interested in education. After twenty years, Ryerson was once again on circuit. Large audiences turned up and the tour was so successful that it was followed by four others over the next twenty-two years.

Altogether, 1847 was a notable year. The first Normal School in Canada West was started in what had been the ballroom in the old Government House in Toronto. It flourished and in 1852 moved to its own

The Toronto Normal and Model Schools, Toronto, 1868

building which included a Model School. Important to the Ryerson family was the birth in July of a son, Charles Egerton (Charley), who lived to have children of his own. He became, as Ryerson had written of his eldest son, "the subject of so many anxious cares and fond hopes."

At the beginning of the following year the first issue of the *Journal of Education* appeared, founded, edited and paid for by Ryerson. He had been thinking about a magazine of this kind for some years, as a means of publicizing his ideas and keeping in touch with superintendents and teachers. Reports on new educational developments abroad were one of its most interesting features. During the first five years Ryerson continued to bring it out at his own expense; for the remaining twenty-five of its existence, the government paid.

The thorny subject of textbooks was not solved by the 1846 Act, which came down heavily against the use

George Brown, founder and editor of the Globe. *He was murdered in 1880, two years before Ryerson's death, by a man he had fired*

of "foreign" — that is, American — books. Ryerson had been very much impressed by the national series he had seen in Ireland; the books were graded, cheap and undenominational. The publishers gave permission for them to be printed in Canada West, and they were gradually introduced into the schools. George Brown, editor of the recently founded *Globe,* was violently opposed to Canadian students using these books. Ryerson retorted that Brown wanted the monopoly of textbooks for his brother-in-law Thomas Nelson, of the publishing house of that name.

It is scarcely strange that in a long and controversial life Ryerson made many enemies, but he certainly had his share of militant Scots. Brown had come to Canada from Scotland, by way of the United States, in 1844. He was a vehement Radical and, to him, Ryerson was still the "turncoat," the "traitor" that he had been to William Lyon Mackenzie and many others in the thirties.

What rankled most, however, was that he was now a successful traitor, a part of the Establishment, the governor-general's pet. Brown's opposition to everything Ryerson said and did became almost pathological. When Ryerson set out on his propaganda tour of the province, Brown published the itinerary and urged as many people as possible to attend the advertised meetings "to show Dr. Ryerson that they are closely watching the efforts he is making to introduce the Prussian system of Education into Canada."

Unlike the majority of Ryerson's other adversaries, Brown never mellowed into an admirer, far less a friend. But he too grew to recognize the value of what Ryerson was trying to do, and slowly the *Globe's* policy moderated. As late as 1872, however, the editor of the *Guardian* wrote: "The Globe is suffering from one of its periodic attacks of Dr. Ryerson on the brain."
The Second Common School Act of 1850 carried Ryerson's plans further. It brought the grammar schools under the control of the Board of Education. More important, it also made taxes on property, to be used for education, the law of the land. Individual school boards, however, still had the choice of obtaining funds by this method or raising the money

by voluntary subscription. Because of its financial provisions, this Bill went a long way towards Ryerson's ultimate goal: free and compulsory education at elementary and secondary levels. It took him another twenty years to achieve this.

The governor-general of Canada for eight of these important years in the history of Canadian education was Lord Elgin. Young, intellectual and enlightened, he was genuinely committed to the welfare of Canada and enjoyed the company of interesting Canadians. Elgin and Ryerson worked well together. Ryerson praised the governor-general highly by describing him as "exceedingly well versed in systems of Education, and a thoroughly practical man on the subject."

In the fall of 1850, Ryerson again went to Europe to buy books and school equipment. He no longer knocked at doors. They opened for him. Elgin gave him a formal letter of introduction to Earl Grey, the Colonial Secretary. In another, private, letter, Elgin wrote: "By this mail one of the ablest men in Canada goes to England, the Revd Dr Ryerson, Superintendent General of Education. . . . I believe he knows as much of Canada as any man."

Within a month, Grey's reply arrived: "Since I last wrote you I have seen both Mr. Macdonald and Dr Ryerson and I have had them to dinner to meet Lord Lansdowne [Chairman of the Privy Council Committee on Education] and C. Wood [Sir Charles Wood, Chancellor of the Exchequer]. . . . Dr Ryerson strikes me as being a very superior man. . . ."

"Mr. Macdonald" was John A. Macdonald, attorney-general of Canada West from 1854 to 1862 and, after Confederation, Canada's first prime minister. Ryerson and Macdonald got along well, and their friendship extended beyond official duties.

John A. Macdonald

In 1855, Ryerson again went abroad to buy books and works of art for a departmental library and an educational museum, both opened the next year. The museum became one of Toronto's big attractions. He spent $4,000 on pictures and statues in Holland. In Germany he bought small models of agricultural equipment and suits of old armour.

Ryerson was necessarily involved in the separate schools controversy. Although he always maintained that without unity there could be no education system, he considered that parents had the right to have their children educated at the schools of their choice. Today Roman Catholics are chiefly associated with separate schools, but in Ryerson's time, before the assimilation of immigrants, language as well as religion played a part in the demands for separate schools.

Indian parents and those speaking Gaelic and German did obtain separate schools, which gradually disappeared with the country's growing sense of national unity. In response to requests from Negro parents, Ryerson was responsible for establishing separate schools for Negro students. A special clause in the Act of 1850 provided for them. (Interestingly enough, on this subject the "reactionary" Strachan was for integration.) Gradually these very specialized schools died out.

Another vital topic that absorbed Ryerson was the equality of the universities. King's College, founded by Strachan and with the lion's share of the cash, had been taken over by the government in 1850 and renamed the University of Toronto. Meanwhile, the Wesleyan Victoria College (which in 1865 became Victoria University), the Presbyterian Queen's, and the Roman Catholic Regiopolis at Kingston also wanted a share of the huge income from the university lands. It was the Clergy Reserves situation all over again. The whole troublesome question involved Ryerson in much disagreeable and wearing effort and was not settled until after his death.

By 1870, public opinion in Ontario* was ready for free schools. In that year almost 100 per cent of the school sections had already voluntarily adopted local taxation. The time was ripe for the School Act of the following year. This major Bill incorporated all the basic principles of the present Ontario school system. For the first time school attendance was made compulsory for at least four months each year for seven- to twelve-year-olds. The old British-inherited grammar schools were renamed high schools. The system was so firmly founded and worked so well that other English-speaking provinces in eastern Canada, some of them pioneers in education, later adopted the Ontario scheme.

The Province of Ontario came into being in 1867 with Confederation

In a great fighting speech, Ryerson once said: "I have sought . . . to ask myself what I could do most for my country's welfare, and how I could contribute most to found a system of education that would give to Canada when I should be no more, a career of a splendour which will make its people proud of it." He succeeded in doing just that.

Egerton Ryerson in middle age

Paterfamilias Chapter 8

Not surprisingly, Ryerson, who had played a father's part in obtaining education for all the young people of the province, was a most loving father to his own children. Of the three, time has closed over Lucilla, the daughter of his first marriage. Strict Methodists gossiped because Ryerson sent her for a while to a convent school in Montreal to learn French; there was more talk later when she and Sophia attended a school in Toronto that taught dancing. When Lucilla was fifteen and her father was away from home on business he was annoyed by delays in forwarding her letters. They were so important to him that he asked his assistant at the Education Office to see that in future "Miss Lucilla's" letters were sent to him by the earliest mail. Two years later, she died of tuberculosis. A servant at the Education Office noticed "the Dr. being in such grief that he had lost himself."

At the time of Lucilla's death, Sophia was thirteen and Charley two. When Sophia was fifteen she had a long illness, and for a time her parents were afraid that she too would die. When she was nineteen, she accompanied her father on his visit to Europe. While he was collecting pictures, she spent some time at a school in Paris to perfect her French and learn the ways of a wider world than the one she had known so far. When Ryerson travelled to Italy, she went too. While in Rome, Ryerson had the opportunity of being presented to the Pope. He took Sophia and one of her friends with him to the audience. After he and the Pope had talked in French for about a quarter of an hour:

Which pope received Ryerson and Sophia and why was his papacy important?

" . . . His Holiness turned to the young ladies (each of whom had a little sheet of note paper in their hands) and said, "My children, what is that you have in your hands?" The girls curtsied respectfully, and told His Holiness that they brought these sheets of paper in hopes His Holiness would have the condescension and kindness to give them his autograph. He smiled and wrote in Latin the benediction: 'Grace, mercy, and peace from God our Father, and Jesus Christ our Lord,' and then kindly gave them also the pen with which it was written."

Amelia Harris, Ryerson's first cousin and Sophia's mother-in-law, was born in 1798 in Upper Canada

Sophia Harris

Edward Harris

Ryerson wrote this account years after. If the secret had leaked out at the time, all Protestant Upper Canada would have been up in arms.

As it was, the Ryerson family were in trouble with their new minister. In a frigid letter, he acknowledged a note from Ryerson with "much pleasure . . . especially because of the assurance it contained that neither Mrs. Ryerson nor yourself were at the Gov. Genls. Ball. Had the assurance included the name of Miss Ryerson, also, it would have been still more valuable." He then expressed his displeasure at the Ryersons' irregular church attendance. Ryerson accepted the reprimand but for "Miss Ryerson" it was the end. She later became an Anglican.

In 1860, Sophia married her second cousin, Edward Harris. He was the grandson of Colonel Samuel Ryerse, whose daughter Amelia had married Captain John Harris of the Royal Navy. He had died ten years before but the Harris family still lived in the big house, Eldon Hall, that he built in London, Ontario. Edward and Sophia made their home there too. To lose a daughter to a husband was in the nature of things and to be expected, but to have her living in another town, 114 miles off, was a severe blow. Ryerson missed her badly. The house was empty without her—and her piano-playing. He was already involved in a prodigious correspondence concerning his work but from the time of Sophia's departure almost until his death a steady stream of letters passed between them.

There is no doubt that Sophia was the love of Ryerson's life: " . . . you—the most thought about and the most beloved of all beyond the limits of home, and perhaps not excepting home itself." Agreeable, quick, clever, fond of books and music, she shared many of her father's interests and was his closest friend. He could tell her things that he would not have mentioned to anyone else. Mrs. Ryerson, on the other hand, with her many good qualities, had the somewhat narrow interests to be expected of a typical minister's wife of the time: her family, including the Armstrong relatives; household affairs; church functions, and the chitchat of friends. She also possessed to a remarkable degree the ability to infuriate her husband. In a letter to Sophia that he asked her to burn, Ryerson burst out how worried he was about Charley's future: that, just as she had when Sophia was small, "your Mamma" would interfere every time he corrected the child or tried to discipline him. His wife's incessant contradicting, nagging (he had a bad time when he lost his money purse), and love of gossip were unbearable. "I feel, at times, desolate beyond what I can express."

Luckily, Ryerson had a refuge. On his father's death in 1854, he inherited a small island off Long Point which became known as Ryerson's Island. It was some thirteen miles from Port Ryerse, not far from where he was born. At Port Ryerse, Ryerson built himself a skiff in which he rowed on Lake Ontario and to and from his island. Here he had a cottage built where he could stay and work peacefully for a week or more. On the island he was able to hunt, for which he had a passion; he had not touched a gun since he was a boy, 40 years before.

Ryerson was a crack shot, and regularly reported his bags of ducks and geese. Once, he told Sophia with pride, using a new breech-loading gun, he shot six ducks on the wing in succession without missing one. When he was over 70, Ryerson killed from seventy to eighty ducks in one day. One night when he was 77, he was unable to get back to the cottage before dark. So, rolling himself in blankets, he slept peacefully in his boat in the marsh. In the morning he shot nine geese. Mrs. Ryerson did not care for all this shooting and sailing. She thought her husband was too old for such pastimes. "Besides I do not think it looks well for a minister to be sporting so much of the time."

Ryerson was entirely fearless in his boat. He thought nothing of crossing Lake Ontario by himself whatever the weather. As Charley got older, his father enjoyed taking him along. One April day when he was returning alone from the island, he ran into ice on the lake. The only thing to do was to row forward in the hope of finding a path away from the wind and the waves which were dashing over the skiff. The broken ice would have cut up the boat in minutes. He then found an ice bank and managed to clamber onto it and draw the skiff after him. The force of the wind was so great that Ryerson hoisted his sail, but he could no longer hold the boat. So he jumped into it and,

Mrs. Egerton Ryerson

steering with his spear, allowed the gale to blow him briskly over the ice to land. He arrived soaked and almost frozen. Even he realized that he had been in great danger. Another time while crossing the lake, he survived a gale so strong that it blew down a church steeple in Toronto.

In 1862, Ryerson became sick and never entirely regained the exceptional strength that he had always enjoyed. (His anxiety over the breakdown of Sophia's marriage, which occurred at the same time, may have contributed to his illness. Edward and Sophia were separated for two years.) After this, he suffered more and more from agonizing headaches, accompanied by temporary blindness, which were brought on by any

Ryerson's Island

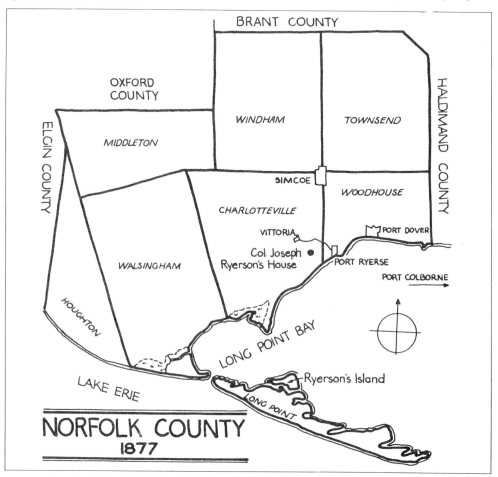

mental overexertion or by overexcitement. Within one
bad week he had three attacks. The only relief was
hard physical exercise and the isolation of the island.
He explained that he travelled as much as possible by
skiff, since on the railway he was certain to meet
friends and acquaintances who would talk to him
about work. When in Toronto, he also rode on
horseback from six to eight every morning. As he got
stronger, he became a great walker.

Ryerson also reported colds, sore throats and
backaches. Once, when he was suffering from boils,
the Roman Catholic Bishop Lynch happened to call.
They talked of many interesting and amusing things.
The painful subject of boils came up. Lynch, from his
own experience, prescribed port wine. He did more
than that: a few days afterwards he sent a dozen
bottles of "the best and most invigorating Port" that
Ryerson had tasted for a long time. Her father had a
little joke with Sophia: the Roman Catholics in the
province would be reassured about their educational
rights by his drinking the wine he had been given.

Ryerson told Sophia everything. She knew when
the double windows were put up and the fuel and
furnace made ready for winter. He wrote that the drain
was blocked; a room was being repapered; a new cook
had arrived (Ryerson, who took pleasure in his meals,
was knowledgeable about cooks and their wages). He
also acted as messenger and postman. He sent her
French books and magazines to encourage her to keep
up her French. She repaid him by writing him a letter
in French; he was delighted and replied in the same
language. A stream of parcels went to London: plants
from the garden; gloves; home-made plum preserves; a
bonnet; German grammars; a recipe from her mother.
When the Speaker gave Ryerson some "nice note
paper," it followed the rest.

Ryerson also received endless requests: to buy a
carriage; have a ring repaired; order a cloak from the
dressmaker; forward a music stand. He did jib once,
however, over clothes for the twin children of Sophia's
sister-in-law. " . . . I am not skilled in the department
of babies' wardrobes, though I should like to see &
kiss the babies themselves."

When he went abroad in 1866, he was expected to

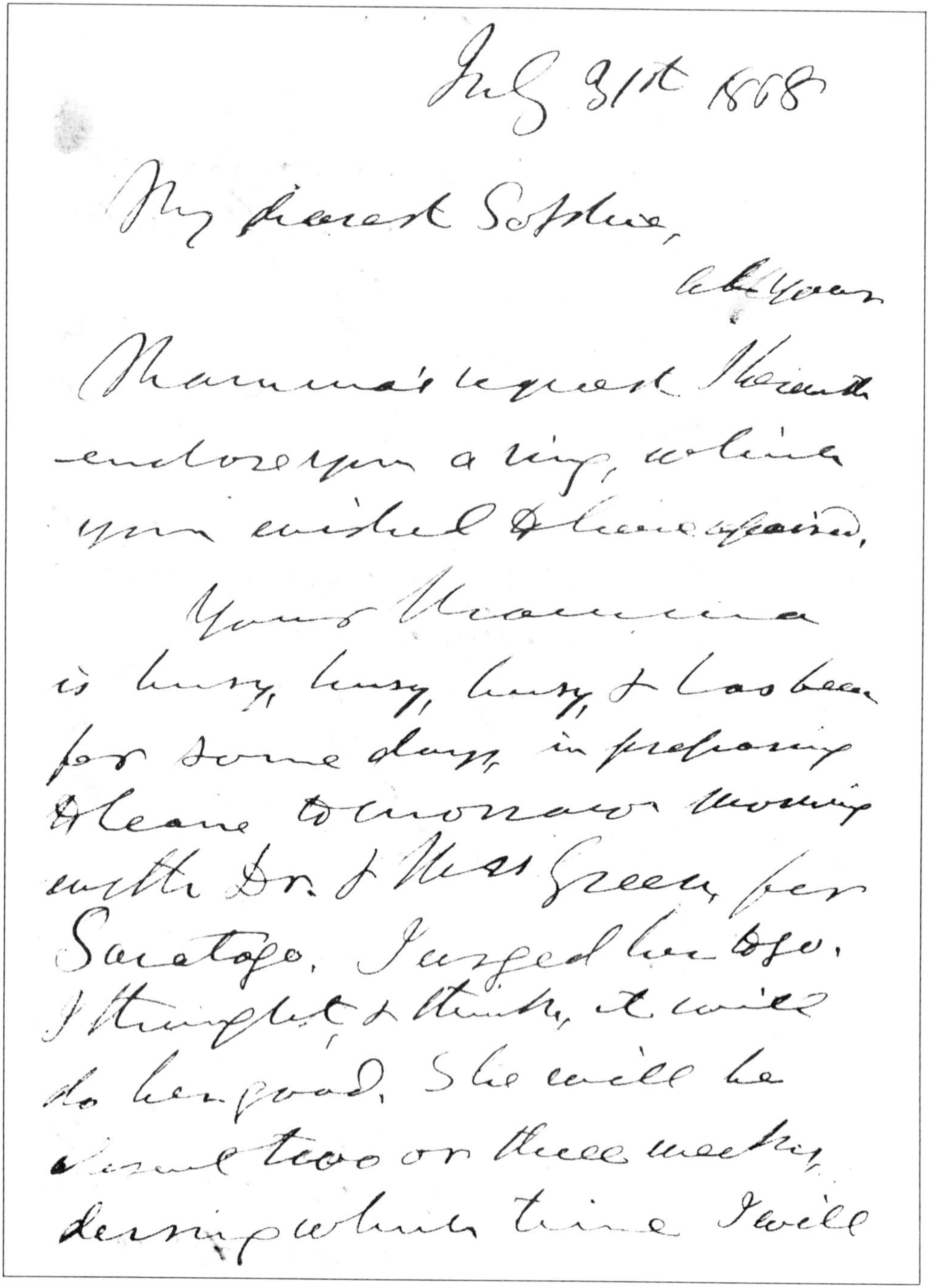

July 31st 1868

My dearest Sophie,

At your Mamma's request I herewith enclose you a ring, as in your wished & have spoiled,

Your Mamma is busy, busy, busy & has been for some days, in preparing to leave tomorrow morning with Dr. & Mrs. Green, for Saratoga. I urged her to go. I thought, & think, it will do her good. She will be gone two or three weeks, during which time I will

The beginning of a letter to Sophia from her father

report on Paris fashions ("Crinoline seems at a discount in the Grande Monde."), and to send samples of Italian silks. Ryerson was commissioned to buy his "dearest Sophie" some dresses in Genoa. One, made of velvet, cost $100, a great deal of money. Although she had asked for this, he decided to give it to her for Christmas. Not all the giving was on his side. Sophia sent her father a flannel undershirt that she made herself, which was "a great comfort", and embroidered a cushion cover for her mother.

Who was responsible for the new look of Paris in 1866?

Sophia was always forgetting things. Her father had to send on a gold ring and bracelet which had been found in the bureau of her room. Another time, when she and Edward stayed at a hotel, Ryerson reassured her that her hatbox and umbrella had been safely retrieved. As for Charley, on one visit to his aunt and uncle in Cobourg he managed to leave behind his flannel shirt, nightgown and bathing towel.

Charley developed into a fine fellow. Naturally, his parents worried about his health. When he was fourteen, "extremely ill" with a severe cold, his father wrote, "I am afraid of his lungs." The following Christmas, having had another cold and a bad cough, he was sent to spend the vacation with his sister. Ryerson was still worried and asked Sophia to get her own doctor to examine Charley. The doctor sent a reassuring message: Charley's lungs were fine; his only trouble was "being coddled." This diagnosis caused gales of laughter at the New Year's Day family party at the Ryersons. Mrs. Ryerson did not laugh.

Ryerson would have liked to send Charley to school in England, to get him right away from his mother, but she would not hear of it. So the boy remained in Toronto, and after a disappointing start (he had to stay in the first grade of the Model School for two years), did well at the Anglican Upper Canada College. He decided to be a barrister and in 1866 he passed both the law and university matriculation examinations. At the end of that year he went with his father on a European tour, as Sophia had done at the same age.

The trip started in London where, apart from the usual tourist attractions, as a special privilege they visited the Bank of England. Charley was fascinated by the gold bars and was allowed to handle them. Each was worth $800. They also packed in visits to the waxworks, a concert, the theatre and the opera. While in London, Ryerson called on the Foreign Secretary who gave him letters of introduction to the British ambassadors at the capitals of each country they were to visit.

Paris captivated Charley, and Ryerson was amazed at the beautiful new houses and boulevards that had been built since he had last seen the city. They went to all the places that Sophia had seen, and often visited the theatre. After this burst of gaiety, the Ryersons went to stay with a family so that Charley could learn French and attend lectures at the university. Ryerson

Charles Egerton (Charley) Ryerson as a student

was pleased with his progress although he complained that his son still did not understand the meaning of work. He told Sophia that, if he wanted to, Charley could learn French more easily and quickly than she had been able to, but that she had had much more perseverance and ambition. For his own part, at his age he had had more than enough of sightseeing; he had undertaken the trip purely for Charley's sake, and it was up to him to make the most of it. It would cost him $1,800 but was money well spent.

From France they went to Italy: first to Rome, then to Naples. In Naples they called on Lord Elgin's sister-in-law. She should have known better than to smile at Charley and ask Ryerson if that was the little boy he had when she was in Toronto. They came back by way of Switzerland and Paris, where Charley remained until the fall. His father arrived home in time to spend a quiet first Dominion Day with his wife.

Ryerson and his son had always been good companions. Charley admired his father and wished to please him. This he certainly did. From his university days, Ryerson had nothing but praise for his son. He worked very hard at college and was "always most exemplary and affectionate." The Christmas after their tour, Ryerson told Charley that he did not know what to buy him, but that "he had my whole heart . . . " That must have been the best present of all.

Chapter 9 "A Great Tree"

Over the years, Ryerson had had his ups and downs with the Methodists too. That was now all past. In 1874, at the General Conference in Toronto, he was elected its first president, the highest honour the church could give. There were no nominations, so Ryerson knew nothing about it until he heard his name announced. As he stepped up onto the platform, all the ministers rose to their feet and cheered him again and again. In those cheers the old man heard the denial of all the lies that had been written about him; the recognition of his great work; the respect, admiration and affection of those whom he had always called brothers. It was the proudest day of his life.

In 1876, after 32 years at the Education Office, Ryerson retired. "Retired" is the wrong word. He just changed his work. On his seventieth birthday, spent alone at the cottage, he had begun his autobiography and he added to it from time to time for the rest of his life. As early as 1860 he had told Sophia that he intended to write a history of the United Empire Loyalists. As soon as he was free, he went to England for six months to research in the British Museum Reading Room in London. Study had always been "meat & drink" to him; thus occupied, he was completely happy. Four years later, in 1880, *The Loyalists of America and Their Times* was published in two volumes.

The situation at home had improved wonderfully. After Ryerson had heard his wife telling Charley in the next room — but meaning her husband to hear — that she wished he would stay on the island for ever, there was a showdown. With Charley's help, the Ryersons made it up and afterwards led a much happier life. Far from exiling him to the cottage, Mrs. Ryerson spent three happy vacations there alone with him, and her husband was able to speak of his last years as "the calm evening of a long and stormy life."

In 1875, Charley married his cousin Lillie Beatty, the daughter of one of his mother's sisters. Both Ryerson and his wife were very fond of Lillie, and Mrs. Ryerson was glad of the companionship of another woman. The next year a grandson, George Egerton, was born, the darling of the family. His brother, Edward Stanley, arrived three years later.

In July of 1881, Ryerson spent two happy weeks with his wife on his beloved island. He did not fish or shoot and they travelled by steamship. It was his last visit. On February 19, 1882, Egerton Ryerson died of pneumonia.

The day afterwards, the *Globe* published an obituary framed in heavy black mourning bands. On the day of the funeral the bells of the Anglican St. James' Cathedral tolled with all the others, and the Legislature adjourned so that the Speaker and members could attend the service. The lieutenant-governor and ministers of every denomination were among the 3,500 people in the church. Bishop (now Archbishop) Lynch called to see Mrs. Ryerson during the day.

On the following Sunday there were memorial services in the big Metropolitan Methodist Church. The evening sermon contained a tribute that was not reported at the time but so impressed one member of the hushed congregation that it has survived. The speaker compared Egerton Ryerson to "a great tree of the forest whose branches raked the passing clouds so that men could only guess at its height; but when it had fallen then could they measure its true proportions."

Ryerson's autograph, 1880

Further Reading

Dickens, Charles. *American Notes.* (Chapters I and II for an amusing first-hand account of the horrors of a transatlantic voyage from London to Halifax, Nova Scotia, in 1842; the last pages of Chapter XIV for Niagara; the first part of Chapter XV for Canada West and Montreal.)

Edwards, Maldwyn. *The Wesley Family and Their Epworth Home.* Manchester: Penwork (Leeds) Ltd., 1972.

Haddal, Ingvar. *John Wesley.* London: The Epworth Press, 1961.

Johnson, F. Henry. *A Brief History of Canadian Education.* Toronto: McGraw-Hill, 1968.

Ryerson, Egerton. *The Story of My Life.* Toronto: William Briggs,* 1883.

Sissons, C.B. (ed.) *My dearest Sophie, Letters from Egerton Ryerson to his Daughter.* Toronto: The Ryerson Press, 1955.

Thomas, Clara. *Ryerson of Upper Canada.* Toronto: The Ryerson Press, 1969.

*It was the custom for the Methodist Book Concern to put the name of the current book steward on their imprint. Ryerson's autobiography therefore was published by the Methodist Book Concern.

Credits

The author is indebted to Dr. Robin S. Harris, University of Toronto, and Mr. Glen Lucas, Archivist, United Church Archives, for their interest and generous permission to use copyrighted material. She is also grateful for much kindness and help from Miss Edith G. Firth, Head, Canadiana and Manuscripts Section, Metropolitan Toronto Central Library; Mrs. Susan Gowan, Cedarbrae Library, Scarborough; Mrs. Jeannette Harkin, Assistant Archivist, Methodist Archives and Research Centre, London, England; Mr. Arthur Steven; Miss Margaret Van Every, Picture Archivist, Archives of Ontario; and Mr. William Yeager, Curator, the Norfolk County Historical Society.

The publishers wish to express their gratitude to the following who have given persmission to use copyrighted illustration in this book:

The Reverend Dr. Maldwyn Edwards, page 8.
Dr. Robin S. Harris, pages 46, 50, 51, 56.
Methodist Archives and Research Centre, page 7.
Metropolitan Toronto Library Board, pages 1, 11, 12, 17, 28, 32, 38, 44.
The Norfolk County Historical Society, page 4.
Ontario Archives, frontispiece, pages 16, 27, 39, 43, 45, 48, 59.
Ontario Department of Lands and Forests, pages 2.
Public Archives of Canada, page 14.
United Church Archives, pages 3, 10, 20, 21, 22, 23, 24, 30, 33, 35, 37, 54, 60.

Editing: Sheba Meland
Design & Cover Illustration: Jack Steiner

The Canadians

Consulting Editor: Roderick Stewart
Editor-in-Chief: Robert Read

Every effort has been made to credit all sources correctly. The author and publishers will welcome any information that will allow them to correct any errors or omissions.